praxie 1972/2:
"Resistance"

2006

it's folly

ly adult-like

sideways, sidewise,
side-winder

a-swirl (you might say)

meadow's
hid grasses.

combined with spoils

ce to royalty

epting, de grace

en plein air

the chamber
of indifference

ming thought
not be stopped;

a workshop, all the f
pages, the green
fires, s

let n

t-like

sideways

side-

w's

a-swif

asses.

combine

yalty

de grace

en plei

EMANATIONS

EMANATIONS

fluttertongue 6

Steven Ross Smith

BookThug 2015

The production of this book was made possible through the generous assistance of the Canada Council for the Arts and the Ontario Arts Council. BookThug also acknowledges the support of the Government of Canada through the Canada Book Fund and the Government of Ontario through the Ontario Book Publishing Tax Credit and the Ontario Book Fund.

LIBRARY AND ARCHIVES CANADA CATALOGUING IN PUBLICATION

Smith, Steven, 1945–, author
    Emanations : fluttertongue 6 / Steven Ross Smith. – First edition.

Poems.
Issued in print and electronic formats.
ISBN 978-1-77166-152-2 (PAPERBACK).–ISBN 978-1-77166-153-9 (HTML).–
ISBN 978-1-77166-154-6 (PDF).–ISBN 978-1-77166-155-3 (MOBI KINDLE)

    I. Title. II. Title: Fluttertongue 6.

PS8587.M59E63 2015   C811'.54   C2015-905693-4
                                      C2015-905694-2

PRINTED IN CANADA

For Jill and Emmett

*their ways with words
and their laughter*

curtains flutter
huffed open
to the light's feint

l'art de la poésie qui décontenance le poèmes

—Michel Deguy

CHIRRUP

On a long thin frond beside an ambling feeder stream
    green frog gleams, sheen and
        pock, journey-scarred

Shiny squatter
    vaults on coil-sprung legs, plays
        hide-and-seek in a camouflage of reeds

That shine is not word-polish
    is slick that slides
        metric feet beyond the edge

Watch out, don't slip
    on thin polytrichum moss
        into carnivorous froggie's watery home

Swamp's warbling orchestra
    is poet's weighty inspiration
        sounding syllables, croak for croak, into twilight

A frog, nonetheless, is not a poem
    though a poem may *have legs*, may leap
        —the poet has witnessed—the frog-leg flip from pond to plate

Toil cast in the skein of words nets scant reward, bares
    verser competition, fish-tale envy, moans of woe
        —*frog ate my living bait*

Chirrup strums another species
    singing harmony from foggy hollows
        rubbing scrawny sonic legs

Meanwhile, back in the bog, pulsing overtone
    persists, a throaty concerto trebles air
        as poet strives for voice to sing along

Poet dons amphibian disguise
    plashes among watery progenitors, splashes
        to and fro, treads here and there, for a line

Poet flails in the pool of words
    noun-croaker, verb-
        stroker, with undertrained legs

Dear customer, we apologize, despite best efforts the poem is unavailable in
    anticipated form—ingredients *anura* and *rhapsodist*
        have leapfrogged, beyond control, to pond's most reedy reach

One by one, one to one, one next to one
    each one amidst the many, all one
        strive and struggle on one thin frond

RUSH

Existence is binary
full of coincidence
and weather

2 hands, 4 hands, sunblast, thunder
on/off
2 I's clutch, palm on palm
palm on juicy raindrops
duck beneath a gallant cloak, umbrella-arc
duck-dash for door-dark mystery
twist the slippery knob
this way, that
left, right

Step, outside 2 inside 2 inside job's compulsion
in2 room's towel
on
         off

            rub absence, ruff

Acquiescence
finds
    fondles, animal
    friction
        1 to 1, 2 to 1
    loosens in the old-new room, tongues

    uncharge/recharge, words
    reflect
        connect

each makes other
                    possible
                    bone holds flesh
                    flesh 2 flesh
                    flesh 2 God
                    God 2 beyond
                    bond 2 here
                    hereness holds 2 tare

                    Holy-hands mould
                    pare

                    pair 2 shape
        maker or made?

I's come
hand-led in shadows
blind, all-seeing hands, tip, turn, on, slip
limb-vines
                    entwine
2gether
                        on/off
                coil/un/coil
                incant

Want that can/t be
                    hide/unhide

Sill mud-clumped
                    bare floor, a foot put there
                            imprint bare, arch- and toe-wet
                                    pool, 2

vapour
2 puddle of light

What's 2 be is
being done
undone

TAILWIND

i.

Spirit, humility—
abstract nouns unfit for poetry
        should reign

Who guards the rivers when
whiskey pours?

Spit, hum

        No one will die, will they?

Forget lumbrous giants
of the Pleistocene
hidden in shale, yet
shaped in plastic figurines

No, do remember, make your mind a museum shop

        Today, on the way, it's double-hitched-lugger-
        eighteen-wheelers-backdraft-tailwind-flaplash-
        gravel-spitter-growl-grille-swaying-thunderers

Every shift has consequence
looming on the out-of-sight horizon

A hit, a pit
a plume

By water, by air
whence come poisons to the feeding tube?

Let's don full hazard gear, with bowed heads

Let those who love, those of spirit, take to boats
take to streams that flow with dark ooze, black
with so much red, so red with black cast
               the red-black spill
               spilled blood

Let's drift from source to mouth
before the river scabs
before nouns go politic
before nouns go polymer
before the nouns go Pollyanna

ii.

A pressed lavish to-do, Papal guardians deal river-front aggravation
   atelier passed over sewers seasoned, solely, finally, a few near isles

Jay-tail in Maugham's shoes, a lesser resident parcels tons of money, laughing
   says a title eaten during the tour, destined for the soirée

Rouge is sent along ideal auto's route in a plein air *gimme*
   eight-part pliant label, bats meant dazed eyelids, wise *ohs* turned insular

Say, come sailing, Graces assert over dances, larch is revered
   a tufted antler poised on scuttled relic

Leave ova, engage in radioed toots, soon viewed, lace, file, and recuse
   touché, tiny damsel, a sanitary veer, a ruse

SLIP

You lose syllables
        (an elegant table
        of elements
        whose fragments go
        periodic)

once-savoured conversations slip

Tongue hosts hesitation, caesura
an instant draws wide
its volumes, mere air   love splits in it

Where you once flexed it, furrowed
                it, it falls
slips from once-rich soil, becomes brittle, crust of another
                    its scooped-out weight

You shed, hollow out, identity dissembles
armies, on both sides in shambles, neither
innocent

Who claims possession?

Wordless
        stasis abrades love to smithereens
    what you knew
        you lose
        again

In the keen heart, a grating ache
a snap-lock prison-gate ache
a throated speechless gasp, everything
rides that air

Everything
        but you
                escapes

ZIGZAG

Feet on soil and grass
scuff the path
toward a poplar bluff
a beckoning of leaves

You zig and zag
not used to this topography
—oh for gin and tonic pause
to steady awkward gait

You'd swallow fear
fear that bares your loneliness

You'd mime a version of yourself
from out's side, ride
inside a gesture's
poise (as in a mist)

You'd blur your misery with lime distraction

The pronoun shifts
on cocktails of sketchy science
engineering of the ether

A leaf can touch your awe

You pray
to save the forest's soar
or turn an eye to score
the canopy, the floor

The rough and scoured overburden sags
understoryed truth's yin and
yang, our reluctance to bow to
unknowing's bent bough

Leaf waves, seems
to greet us, leaf
twists on its thin
stem, contorts, on its thin
thin stem

OXYGEN

Walk soil's trodden layer between here
and hereafter

Slog with
or without ailment's
endless familiar list

Above the field, a red
-tailed hawk, on meal
-watch
drifts

In praise
peer for the root of poetry
weighed with gun-bled body count
the endless memoriam

Ache for a word
say, *savoir*
to take to the tongue, to savour
taken by needle or flute, whatever tool
whatever drug, what-
ever saviour soothes

One to one, or many to many, all
humanity's breath bubbles up
to the stratosphere, falls silent
as oxygen thins, no
breath to praise
to keen

Below, footsteps parade
echo, fade, alchemical
shift
    in clockless
           infinite
                unpredictable weather

SLENDER

Surge and glide
prow-pushed ripples
silken billowing
a glimpse of flow

Slip, slick
night's moon-green
sheen, wet in
oar-trail, light-
headed allure
stir of aquatic star-
burst, molecular agi
tation, bio
        lumin
            escence

On mysterious light
the unstable world
floats its
erasings

A slender hull
patterns the channel
words drift
floating filaments
fore and aft, port and star-
board, oar-dipped, stell-
ar dazzle
trailing the

blade

Bloom
ommmmm
and de-
cay

Time sieved
from the flittering
eye

LADEN

i.

WHU   what was that?

Waffle, whisper, a nothingness   across
           jet of air   jet stream
       (patience, it will come)
and come\again return of what's not . . .
said
       from a suffering oesophageal
all knowing, all known
wound

Blade-fall   precise, articulate
with blossoms, with blessings, tempered
feathered edge honed at the whetstone
if let, could cut (wing) open the wall
and intemperate temperatures
       sooner, too soon   can be a season a stutter a
           wor(l)d sev-
              erer

We want
       want a better climate (clemency) and
words spurred from a high
           pressure
drop
      a proclamation
to lead us   every (one)
            where

ii.

Firm and before us
and liquid at the same time

   We are builders   broken

Stones can grow from water

   Minerals leeched out
   pocked, weathered, greening
rock stops all approach
       by definition
(what's hidden in run-off—cavern, rift, a
       new solid?—stalactitical)

They swim or crawl there with legs or undulations
or with winged ululations flutter (through, over?
never seen again)
   their tiny lives
          .

Hard-rock, hiding place writes the hill
's arc from beneath the hill's arc
takes the eye there and to horizon, final
   edge
all there is in this place for\hide or\hesitate or\
heave
       'n hard-nosed, you
and me, bent
down against the mineral
taking mineral breath
our fingers, knuckle-skin pale

nails to cuticles, pink
  grip
shaded, laden as we must

It slips
WHU   what was it?

WITNESS

WHOOSH
overhead
    lifts
       your eyes, to wing-flap's call, to
       privilege of witness

Your pursuit of—nothing in particular—
in fir and pine forest
attends to
tail-flick, stick-shape
spins to brush-rustle

You dissect clues with close attention
 stiffen at a twig-snap
      (or was that a tweak in your own bones?)
        forearm hairs stand erect, alert
        wind and shadows entice
        your tuned senses

        What shape, what scent
          feral/mineral?

        What fierce and hungry thing rib-ripples
        in its thin body, creeps
        on meal-watch?

        Movement at the corner of your eye
        —feather-clump, or light-cast stone?—
        and over there among the mottled poplars

—a twitch—
doe as leap
her white-rump flash, a
question mark

Where does she go
where does crow rest?

Are you watched?

Your whisper echoes, slight, in crisp air
honoured to be

so

ASLANT

Bird bodies dart, pepper
dusk's silty light
swallows snack in buggy air
eagle turns a last gyre
day tilts away on its axis

Power-mowers settle
unwind their whines
to undisturb

Poet, a pitch of try-to-understand before dark drops, poet
    un-sparked, probes for confidence, reckons
    among instabilities, allures, while
    low aslant shadows swallow light

    The loving, fearful heart
    stumbles, stutters the page

    The human vertebrae, bent to task, aches
    talks alone, talon-locks on elusive thought

        Owlish swivel-necked night hinges
        its *either-or* or-ness diversions
        divided in *might* or *might-not*

Poet-dreamer bobs
on spectral ribbons of *maybe*

A night-sound knifes—
rock-fall
key-click in cotter?

A syllable incised

What speaks?

Poet, fearful, holds
faith, in the sung shape
of the word for
dawn

WATER-SONG

Skein-snagged, swims, speaks to fish
lured to pools of words

Arm-stroker
determined, away from shallows, fins
downward to depths where darkness bleeds and reeds entwine
down to seed/element/singularity/source
reverent

Murk-flirter
mourns the blessed kernel, the under-
surface rhyme, its toll

Dark-hearer, dark-seer
hears it, sees it
the call of beloved eyes, pierced yet-again
by her always-returning gaze
locked in clock hands
a time-crevasse chime
a choir (quire) in the gulped
latched
instant

Edge-reacher
with ash-laden ink
—sublime and weighted—
empty-handed, unable to rewind time
in his turveyed world
etched, scooped-out, furrowed
wound-mirrored

From-dust-singer
fusses husks of words for musk
scrapes style-clad complacency, pain, snared, in
the chemistry of ink, its stark stain, its sting
snared in shadow, in muck-milk stream
in camp-yard, love-shard

In latch-snap, keyless, gill-less, guilt-pierced, dive-tilt
water-song-wrung, pocket-weighted

Water's blade burrows his lungs
with breath-stealing cleave

REPERTOIRE

See no
hear no
touch no
guile nets
no virtue

In Eco's vertiginous skein
vorticella's one-celled bell
chimes God's repertoire
  wait—equal time for
  Yahweh's way
  Allah's sanction
  Buddha's bodhisattva
Let oneness
ring the heart-centre

  Wariness leans in
  droops cornucopia's
  en-gene-ered glow
  as shade-designed torts
  engender cakewalk patents

Eyes' distorted sitings follow fool forays
foofaraw bouquets that flare
in fracked faucets

Perfect fumables
buck and siphon *safety and security*
owed or owned

tote all counterings
slumps of debt and defeat

Suffering mounts, retorques
                    tor
                -ments
                            tor
                        -tures
                                tar
                            -nishes
                                        niche gashes gnash
                                        in Tar Nation, as

Diners on steak tartar
discuss Terms
of *necessary* terminations
to protect
bucks

GMOdified in-corp-orate
corporated ruinage

Pirated lute line sags, ludic snags

Lustrous lucite's available
for mass consumption

Greasery on snow
slimes the port
stains the retail H_2O

O, nasty quacks are on the loose
DonQ ducks the windmill's flounce and flutter

Sweet Otherly sniffs
fish-carts, wheat-cuts, sweatshops
scent of ages pours through narrow passages
lime cakes nets and hampers
markets bullish as the blueish schools'
full flow diminishes

Snub-nosed bullets vault
haunt a holy Affront, propelled
against the tender hold

Whistling witness wardrobed in the landfill

Morph-ine-serene faces erase

In due course
(all talk)   in due curse's
                   buck-balked play
                   on the lip of
                                scoured, sour graves

            O Oneness

                      What comes?

AGORA

Look over there, clipped to the line, forgotten laundry
blown out of itself—everything pushes, whizzes
whooshes and whiptails—you recall like any other day—
but not really—swaying on the slung blank fingered
map, blown past identity on unproductive gusts eye-
stung, a mirage of smiling ghosts, *F*-word determined to
be heard—its grating vocable

Or amble, a circular arboreal persuasion, a grand
handshake, leaves too, shake, rattle, and roll on stems
probe high toward flickering sunlight, branch out as if
fixated—life needs light—for a beam cast over a shoulder
onto page's holy act

Look closely, despite your silty vision, at colours of
bark in pulsing light—a spectrum of surprises tumbles
Wound's melancholy, it's all open space, angst, agora
of Wound's (let's say "*W*") phobic skinny-leg underpin
shaky on undermined ground

W wants to go back, but the leaves are raked into piles—
which one holds the treasure trove—truce or falsity—in
a moment of distraction, *W* thinks *jack-off,* but it's the
name of a flower he's reaching for, bright, bobbing orange
and red, that eludes, with tendrils that attract even when
tangled or when a rib snaps and repellant cloth droops
and rain soaks head and shoulders, splashes and blotters
up *W*'s trouser cuffs to the knees, nothing spiritual about
that, all sticky, cloying, no reason to be rude, even if

annoyed—it's out of place at finer parties where chatter rolls ideas room to room then out the back door down the lane

W jots—from fabric ribs—fluid lines, loves the way letters roll and tumble—*W* or *You* may not live one hundred years, nonetheless on close inspection will witness the fractioning, the machines' command

Still, insects carry on, bug with biting determination infestation—some are beautiful, even turn *W/You* on with flash-dazzle of understanding or of wing, such is the dominant coupled social order—binary—undeniably

But the bond wanders, unruly with desire, under-understood and pulsing, reaches by fact or fantasy for propriety, realm way out there faster than light than anything we know, not perceptible here, no matter how long you sit still, but it happens, reveals its toll down the road

Got to love the Chinook, its blustery warmth and gravel blast, heady as you get—in the market a hand weighs the purchase, overcharges an unremarkable commodity—a little here, a little there, bit and piece, nickel and dime cookie and crime—truth is slippery, chancy, snake-eyed or lucky-sevened—the poem, yes, even when thick with dense tumbles of letters might get to the quick, just might—the clouded eye—iris blown open, no *Jack* to be seen—wide to a blast of reds and yellows— *W-ow*—eyes' trellised melody trilling the nasturtiums

PENT

i.

Boy+girl+curiosity
three to the third power
mathematics of
flesh, calculating the spread
sheet
opening

—The poem's reception—

Papery musk rises
to senses, on
discovery's plume
radiant bloom of
grass blades, verdant beside the stream
spirited with want
    (their shy fevers)
drinking in
finger-brush of the timeless new
the sacred   the ancient

—Such poem cannot be written—

On young and tender knees
one to another, face to face—in
the chest a starling murmuration
in the belly
earthquakes—

scuffed soil, the parch
lies down to the tickle of grasses

—*The poem unwrites*—

Avid for shining skin
on the unfettered bed
blade-feathered bed
bed of coil and s/
play

ii.

    Repent & keep it zipped! says
        the white-necked, thin-lip

—The poem all ears—

    Sing it like a nursery rhyme
    your sorry palms
    pressed in prayer

—Poem knows the nursery's far behind—

Boy+girl+curiosity
hum, kneeling to un-
collared fever
        arch on the stream's scratchy bank

             Once

       more

               and *again*
      and

SPIDERISH

Z knew Alpha was the start, enough
for blueprint variations

Skeleton-reefs'
intricate organic
design, their minty
whiteness, peleton-shifty comb-
inations, seabone, cyclic
irreplaceable

GEOPHAGY ON THE RISE

Let's build   different binaries
with blocks   whatever looks
squarish   well rectangular then
alright   toss in a flaired swoosh
and we'll go spiderish   crawl
webby geometric bounds   not
for self nor entertainment this
probe   this investigation of
cadavers   a search for authentic
geomantic revelation   choral
riff in hi-tech earbuds in down-
town high-finance skyscrapers
in hygienic suburbs   in clearest
turquoise tropic seas—letter A

REAL ESTATE PRICES SOAR ON WALKABILITY

Up the cortical ante—
Kant cell, held in rapture

(Asides #1, 2, 3)

> *1. His followers—the aforementioned philosopher—*
> *(his web of thought)*
> *(deeper than the self-full randy Rand-ers)*

> *2. Or, to be candid, it's time to drop*
> *—cough, cough—candied Keynes' burred key*
> *and feed the world*

SHED BODY FAT NOW

Theory is inedible. Enough cerebral asides!

> *(3. Even this, an aside)*

We'll read his book—I speak of Zed, his *A*—'til hell
freezes (as they say)—do you think?
(will it, if we warm?)
for the mysteries—to comprehend, 'til pages
go crisp and brittle (will they crumble?)

(Asides #4, 5)

> *4. Our ears grow huge to*
> *take in all the songs expelled on*
> *iTunes, where ova, ungulates, oblates, even*
> *omelettes, sing (calcium shells cast aside)*

FUKUSHIMA RAT CAUSED BLACKOUT

5. Get out there, behind the letter combinations
a sonographer's luck or intention, a
phoneme-ographer's gelled or celled links

He's strung it, thrummed it
uncocooned it to loosen our swoon
all the way to Zed
—he'd say *Zee*—
where the mind of the Zuk
—tunester
taps his feet
his complex chorus
on shining ivories
on shrinking coral quays

PECK

Any poem as in Finnish or finite, oh!

A quiver of carol came in, oh yes
yay garrulous knave
yay girl Annie Vee
extrasensory perception aces returning aunties
various signals slash ear-bats

Hello cement terroirs
a quiver of karaoke lino
yes yay girl, ah, lamb, yoohoo
lamb, you jar, cannot emulate loss
lamb-oochie, rack, emit a dose gal
loosen and succumb, oh!

Lalu's coin, autumn, has lost gallons, yo
lost galleons cannot save, incant, tear, sob
relief appears, oh silly Annie, verse a hoarse voice
to decorate the zone

Phew, deli girl, vie into Ozzie's throw
become a mole, air no hatchet
case of *eau de loge*, my does
tender moss keeps a rot, faces last year's bus, deals on cement areas

Yo bees doze, duller roses
spaghetti desires can terribly end

Space age devil canes Evie

Dowse ninnies' low cost camp
to push, jab any orange dollars, pupils, dumb assassin, oh
per oil dose, no Hasidics' or nuns' cane-numb Eros
Porky, assign angst, gusto, yay
see some bra
Porky, ah, sell a demonstration's
dull doubter, row infinite, OK?

Noise? soya?

Yes, lost mural, lost elm, where to yell, castigate ideals, yeah
now waive resurrection, sin, finally
lost moor to sod, in hell
new marrow doughs, payroll numb arrows
dozers adore, messy, all lasses, smoother

Why come? *hola*
mute hare-tam, elude, lull
ooze time's blade

Landed, a low galosh
while lost gallons
swallow a bent vole on our sober lane of ivy

Tender mosques, peace-signed descants
oh lost verbs
aid lost semen's arias

NORTH

Even in the dark the drag-
line bucket shuffles
clocking chancy operations
over flute and bassoon

Before you
every barb of the *huh*
moans, human nation of
grille-wire fences

The well-appointed room
of public address compass-points
at the unstoppable

In chill, forever
down hugs a chest
each life seeks

Reveals unbalance
as stun-gun anointments
fire revelations out of range

Here a quilt's trills
orient the ear, the light
sun now, so low
lures the scuffle for coin

In holding pens
an ear is chopped
as lips sing

Stares rifle through
chattering counterpoint
north to north's pristine
patient
last geology

Hope holds
its alchemy
a landscape of *where*
revealed

Fenced compounds over there
burlaped, ask dwellers what
botany whispers

A scraper squeal waltzes
carves up protesting tundra
revs up the flung
ka-ching

Sell-off there
a face watches
the *I-Ching* grams default
to cached messages

Over mud-pump-hum-mambo
machine-gun stings
the soft
night-REMs

West, south
to the *Vedas*
to the easterlies
where to look?

A cheek chafes on what's known
a face in the dark, squeezed
in salon's triggered music
of wish
of worry

Always north
and singing of
the glistening

OFFERING

i.

A hand reaches
as if an undreamed-of dream surges from
a wrinkle in prune-dark sleep

throws shadow-startle down a throat
(a gurgle of barks?)
thunder
limbs, reed-like, water-tossed
shudder of tendrils
chokes off the blush of sun
a clutch of fisted throats
a grasp of thin fingers slips, fingers brush   fear
's   Eros   wells

Walls
swells of water tumbling crazed snatch at solid no solid
ground-gone-legless in tumult reeling water unswimmable
dark-pitch wet-whirl moment's nightsweat nightmare-come-real
batters   undoes   unroots   unbattens
obliterates
reclaims

ii.

Sudden
prayer apparent at a lip's (as if
slipped)
moist words

Canny sun
shines or shuns (as if
to challenge)

Branching oxygen machines
stand steady on stern trunks (as if
they know
themselves)

Offering—air, whisper
to vaporous unpredictable clouds (as if
un-cloaking

Prayer) opens
a shelter of leaves (crackle)
a weave of wool (chafes the neck)
a gold rush (in the chest)

Or lances an ache's crush
from lungs to mouth-chamber
over lips
a current of air (as if)
                    involuntary   song

iii.

Handful or hillside of geo-
mantic dirt divines disturbance
(stasis: an assumption of soil)
thrown soil   radiant   with
signs and seams
of loosening   a random carom-crush of mud
used-to-be-root-laced-firmament   unthreaded   untethered   dirt, a

Tossed weight   slumps

Shoulders   swathed   earth, citizens

A surround of trees   leans
teeters with air's and earth's grumble   a stir
(since they are lungs)
some tumble   some

Stand   poised to save (air, soil) from poisonings

As with earth, flesh
(some say we invoke, invite our fates)

Some stand
some   fold   fold in   (Thanatos)

Look for   a sign   a shun
                        uncanny short
                                    -sighted (sight)

This moment   unrooted   (act!)   gone in less than a toss, slides

      Away   but soil   will lurch   again

DIS(RE)COVERY

i. *(scramble)*

The *adventure* of decibels, headlong
production, latchkey, the patchwork
and on any device
material enterprise on foresight
trees on the path, full treasures for *rapid exchange*, for
signage
it would be silly to program

Gilkison achieved peripheral letters, unrecorded
other than the greater benchmark

William recorded scars and the heft, viz. microsoft's mission
and *the 1779–1833* dead founder, down

Reward, the April *seasonal recovery*, be
(would it not?)
place food before the captain anytime, any place and
ave
alongside by the mellifluous gorge
died

Hath smeared Elora in witness
Marks off
past eleven social results to the rapids
k's the me
Geddes Ave., the were, the down

One peace, the no, and carry oft
a hinge walk, sell, empower, *Elora wait for me*
here in ambrosial *i*

ii. *(stealth)*

Foot-
fall, our heavy shoes

Hands, once
flashed the fingered V
sliding letter to a symbol, a word built on vertical
on 'I', letter as cliff, hover-wish, lulls violence, eases love (that itchy
    word)
—scratch it back from the boutique, the Bouncing Betty

Eyes dry
no sight forced, fore-cast
no *making it* made
after trodding, nothing but shoeprint, wing-whoosh
mass-soft song's diminuendo

Elixir-mixed mind
fence removed, litter lingers

Slip in on strip mall's mercantile oil
all the trans jangle, the works
on register's ring, on ring-
tone edges
blot, blur, blurt
loft buried
in bargain time (bargaining for time)
bouquet blooms, plump and puckered
hoist, heft of a poem
attends   an ecology

See, look close, beneath
my petal-sleeves
at my wound, swear
on a Visa card, for eco-tours, for every
finger, every eyeball
in a bone-
bowl

In an earthy hollow
you'll need a boost
a lift to   calculate or
laugh, to compute among mounting or shrinking
snowbanks where
engine-whine prevails

Winter-cold hand
scuffling at a ring of keys

Boney foot, shoe-worn, aching
follows an arrow (vague in clouding eyes)
to the gorgeous
melody of incline
discordant gouge
in geologic time

Notes scrabble, rimed in a pebbly throat, all is
striation above a white churn

iii. *(oxfordized)*

Un-beings without fire flame or glow in this Earth-locale roam on foot among freedoms from or cessations of all war and hostilities caused by a giddy fish or god—hail!— wander by alphabet's eleventh letter locale's illustration of forms and inflections or a perennial plant having a self-supporting woody trunk and riches stored or accumulated periodical recurrent, disposed of by sale

Creator—the number of a single thing without any more—chief or headman a common masculine personal designation also used in the name of certain species of pinks and other flowers, early slang, false keys, his male offspring a fifty-four-year span of man and sentient beings gave up life, in the cruellest month on the anterior side of the complete action of springing back again, of the male's look forward and engagement in a bold arduous or momentous undertaking, won

Absolute absence of high position in a scale of quantitative estimation of return or recompense made to or received by a person for some favour, having or mocking allied presentations, the conjunction expressing the comparative of inequality, the surveyor's mark cut in some durable material, as rock, wall, gate, pillar, face of a building, etc., to indicate the starting, closing or any suitable intermediate point in a line of levels for determination of altitudes over the face of a country

Several times, preserved in writing or other permanent form, one-tenth of the whole ethereal material jumble where one distinct from one already specified or other surface serving to enclose or bound a space or hollow, an aspect or view of beyond, swiftly taken into the system to maintain life and growth—which happens, exciting or remarkable—without design

Movable joint allowing a pivot tool or wedge usually of iron which inserts in a slot and turns to move a bolt backwards or forwards to draw the night-spring-lock for fastening closed a door or gate or opening

Outward part of an organic body characteristic of circumference or external surface smudged alphabetic symbols ponderousness, definite scheme of reciprocal giving and receiving

Visible traces or impressions diversifying a surface vestiges of a healed wound, first-person pronoun conveys while bearing up the infinitive of existence, one who gives evidence on behalf of the accusative and dative form of the first-person pronoun, namely the world's largest software company's effort to convert heathens, to enable by means of magnificent computer operating programs without temporal limit without geographic restriction and above and in contact with all contrivances

Neuter noun, conditional form of being, foolish, deserv-
ing pity, conditional (as above) neuter noun (as above)
negative—except for distinguishing marks, name of
Ontario town and geologic phenomenon

Stay in place in expectation of the accusative and dative
form of the first-person pronoun the first feathering
of young birds or descend over the edge of the sweetly
flowing sweet-as-honey ravine with rocky walls above
and supported by a way beaten down or through or trod
by men or beasts not preserved in writing or musically
rendered and scramble with blind impetuosity toward the
river bed's white rush its steep and gorgeous descent

ALLURE

In letters' allure
a word mistaken
glass for *grass*
grasp lost

In the reach
a flask tumbles

Shards shimmer
a thousand splintered
blades, glitter
bristled over hard tile
to the pan

Penned alchemy
—think Hopkins, word-hurler
torquer, binder of
burls in metric blend

How, in words' terms, to bend, to reassemble
to make-it-up
how to inhale lost word-scent
to go eye-blind
in plot's risky grasp
of the vital neck

Flask
is broken
word de-
cants

Word, all
vapour, woven over you
it sings, *ah-woo-ooo* (this poor imitation)

You toss down a sheet, a white sheen to
muffle the crash, to
cushion hazards, to
swab the scars, to
envelop the puff, to
net the splintered said

DECOY

Sleep's fall through the open frame
into black gone-ness

    In the dream
    I is anyone, someone else
    who chases feigned innocence
    though heart's hiding chafes
    scrapes achy scabs in the dash

    I slackens at a rustle, a leaf-soft shudder
    leaves, subtle as leaves can be, speak
    to a paused, poised ear

    I lightens
    surface tension floats I, a leaf
    a mallard on a pond, just
    for a second

    Lacking feathers, buoyancy
    I panics, treads
    I becomes a decoy, a mute lure with useless wooden wings
    bobbing, hovering so
    far from who I wishes to be

    I's alone
    though from dream-shadow
    eyes stretch toward, to
    read I

Trapped by sheets
I spins
and wrestles
puffs, tongues I's teeth
shouts out one word
that pops open I's eyes
sends them swimming concentric circles through the room

From way outside I's pillow-muffed ears
I hears a choral sound

Echoes of everyone's voices I has known
blowing through shades
across rooms, across
rock, water, through pillows
over lips

Their voices
(I's voice too)
ripple   toward
                    and
            away
and with retreat, a bit of
I's name
grows unfamiliar in their throats

Curtains flutter
huffed open
to the light's feint

TUMBLE

ZI—a triggered
pellet gun—*ZK!*

Poet-about-town startles
grabs his hefty volume
leaps from the bar

When silence returns, poet
peers, ascends to his perch

Poet dreams spring's downpour, noble rain's exultation
that torrents away chill and grit and twig-bunch
Poet calls for warmth, renewal, he sees the phenomenal

> rumblyshiny motorbikes aerodynamic pouchstuffed
> infant strollers pushed by pale legs in skimpy shorts
> canes and walkers propelling stiffjointed seniors
> fraycuffed teens with greenstreaked hair hitherthither
> waveandchat hugandsnuggle toney towny packaged
> rackaged sassyassy zippedydoodah bicepybipedy
> freeforall on boulevard greens filled with arcing
> baseballs beachballs soccerballs boardrolling
> kitesailing springsprouting rubatopulsed human flow

He watches—in The Stadium of Late Capitalism—the pitch, the throes

Poet retreats beyond the track where fields unscroll
where spherical, dried-out, over-wintered weeds tumble
drugged and dragged by wind, over crusted, hungry Earth

Poet toils, seeds his land (stirred by Pound, Monsanto, Kant)
steers his gleaming tractor, cab-sheltered from the scraping wind
hand off the wheel he jots his thought, sketches his longing, his hope
poet breathes his line, Marx
his niche . . . eh?
etches alphabet, correction
                his verse
                in furrows
                in a field
                's soil

LURCH

Beach laced
waste, waist-high
bitten by plastic jagged beads
blandished by platelets jerry-slagged
up from polymer sea
(Lord have mercy)
   stuff a-bob gleams entices incites glissades entraps increases
             brand-game of games
            card-flip tele-spectacle
         gaper captive to the flush of light
      garbage carboniferous in flutter of likeness
       cardiograph-floods telos-speculum

brass-gamma of gamut
two-for-one-today-only-last-chance
the beholder swears by it
buys it wears it
caddies it weeps it
the believer swerves on its pyramid trip
       tips queasy stomach's toss-up in hollow churn
            tilts the quiet stoner
           in a Pyrex triplex flood
        a gush over lives old and newborn
         whose houses sink under bad
          weather bad debt leaky writs

nifty howlers sizzle under balconies
florescence gyrates over lighthouse decisions
"quick pass the broom—just the handle might do"
its skinny buoyancy handy bristles
to float to swiff particulate off the junk to
flourish to swink passé off the jupon

slapstick bureaucracy hard-boiled broadbrim
natty dealer enters the press scrum
hanky-panky dodge
patent shoes tap a brisk drum-step across tile
waft a buffed snare-trail of garb-status
armani mourning jacket cardboard shack

a marked deck
a marsupial decline
attrition sells—everything must go
chin held just so in pause
in poise as if a crown above
a posture lulls as if a crucifixion overhead

with ceremony's banner and bane
postponement and delay
with certificate's banzai and banjo
chinchilla herded just so in pawnshop in pokeweed
all cuffs and gems behind the starch
below starling murmurations

all guff and dirty wrists all the collars sullied
the suit's a ragg'd-up clown
all disarming wrynecks
the diamond card
the ace-in-hand in a blink flicks up a cuff
a hangman cardiology

casino camera-scans feed back through lens
through tinted one-way glass to screens
beside the case of semi-automatic guns
beside the seminal avenaceous gusts
through titillated opalescent gleam
surveillance framed and digitized

paradise is scrutiny
en route through the rubble heap
paragraphs are freed from
poetry's dilapidated sculpture
enshrouded in rubric heartburn
here or there defibrillation's thievery and therapy
                              beside mottled lawns cons bus bombs
                                    bushmaster concession bonanzas
                                 waves grind on the buried beach
                              slough the cabled beadwork debris
                                    spill bloom and decay
                                 the tune of the tide its
stack and retreat stack and retreat treasure and theft
stake and retype rape and repeat
repeal and restake
waves stack and retreat
treasure and theft
treasure and theft

OLIVES

It's always the springy stir
plan, plant, hope
slipped into Earth-skin's slopey pores
(soon to be cellular mirrors)
      glinty, green, spring flares
      sprung from soft mossy pads
as you slice on the chopping board

This truth's a bit musky for most
      (like the unwashed uncle
      invited for fettuccini champignon)

Tsk-tsk or *snicker-snicker* go the guests, or *ah-h* their
claims or denials

Who planted this row? they ask, draining

How lovely

Truth in furrows, in veins
the answer lost
in pasta's kerfuffle

How fresh

Chase around the gleaming glass
spear an olive in a vodka martini
Does it have a red heart?

Soon enough shoots will show

How lush

Leafing out

The membrane is thin, contains all life

How says uncle *al dente*

PETALS

i.

Speak not of flowers, but of Hunger

Know stomach's rage
head-throb attention to the knot
between rattle-ribs
wrung daze, the portable hollow
stench the ache leaks

Hunger'd snack
between *survival* and *survive*
on blood

Hunger, not furtive, not subtle, gnaws
not shadow, not fashion-skinny runways

Hunger's bulge-eyed bodies
eyes going milky for want of milk

Hunger tends lack's shanty, hunts
any morsel, edible or not
an eddy of leaves is soup if water can be found
sand grains aswirl, grits to chew
that scratch voice from the throat

By night, on dream-drift, tongue
licks thick butter, cups sweet nectar
Hunger wakes to a skinny drool

Check Out Receipt

Banff Public Library
403-762-2661

Monday, June 24, 2019 4:50:51 PM
05190

Title: Transient light : poems
Call no.: Canadian SMITH
Material: Book
Due: 15/07/2019

Title: Emanations : fluttertongue 6
Call no.: Canadian SMITH
Material: Book
Due: 15/07/2019

Total items: 2

You just saved $43.00 by using your library.
You have saved $219.89 this past year and
$1,366.33 since you began using the library!

Thank You!

Hunger's eye hazes, pools a cerulean mirage
    a flotilla bearing fruits on a shimmer
    bobbing, delicate as blossom petals
    thin skins adrift, scent soaked up
    beauty limp and fading in the salt

ii.

Hunger is hidden
behind verdant, moist, manicured, owned order
Hungerbody bound
to bone-hard blistered soil, by emptiness

Hungerbody longs for as little as a seed
scavenged in the garbage dump
dug from sand swirl
out of sight of the flyby spy-drone's
                    mission, to map evidence
                    to capture Hunger's impractical fashion
                    its gape
                    its want
                    its parched flesh
                    to steal its dream, the one
Hungerbody dreams over the fence-grille, of
plum trees, of sun flickering on purple flesh, plump and juicy orbs
that beckon tongues

Hungerbody dreams it is
not a dream

GLORY

Remember we were young and charged
        because in the moment reserved just for us
remember we were the best we would be, we
        because knew for sure—or
remember not, we might have been beautiful—or
        because not, we were indestructible

Remember we had time, all time, in one rush, it was
        because the best time, but we knew
remember no comparisons, but we knew
        because uncertainty, we knew, did not know, our skin

Remember we wore our tender bodies
        because fearfully and
remember bravely at the same time
        because on some days with pride
remember our bodies glowed
        because our skin shone where
remember we let it show
        because we were fierce for
remember many reasons

Because we sought the mirror, the mirror
        remember shone with risk, with
because disappointment, hot
        remember needing
because, or
        remember not
because we were in there, out there in

remember the glass, inside
because ourselves, we wanted but
	remember our want lay inarticulate

Because we offered
	remember our longing flesh drew
because eyes and tongues, we offered
	remember our pale, our tan, splendour, dazzled, dazed in
because ripe air, to ones we
	remember thought magnificent, beautiful beyond compare, or
because at least possible, or
	remember—not

Because, yes, those eyes and tongues, we
	remember were stung with, or by
because we rose to glory
	remember at the top of the game
because uncertain of the game
	remember guessing at every step
because at the height
	remember the steep grade

Because we were in the haze
	remember of ourselves
because we were spectres
	remember, expectant
because pent

Remember the heady slick height, it
	because, slipped us up

ARROWS

Poet would love it if poems echoed, choate or in-
shone like sprigs, tentacles of multiplication, earnestly
adult mathematics like mirrored teeth shining white
a bleached smile squared or straw-blonde grasses
unfolding through infinite pure-number spectacles
on spectators in plaid spats or a tawny coyote scuffing
nuzzling in the snow in the now for a meal-deal and
with a leap, a whirl of motion joyous grin, its canines
gripping a vole such instruction—Grace—the coupling
canny defeat of Chaos Theory

But hark, for the rest, fresh greens gleam in the
produce aisle, insistent rhymes cannot be stopped
stalks stocked, a stark appealing thought—sublime—
cocktail break, celery stem and lime in a Bloody Mary
(Mother of a goddam good idea) though contrary
early in the day

Mental evolution almost as much as good looks cashes
value a grab and advantage, more money for stingy
spoilers but not for soil, but cache back to beauty, it
doesn't hurt unless found under scalpel or injection
not natural selection, it's string-folly in the hands of
hustling puppeteers—the displacement-market of
staged difference (a marked note, subprime) sideways
sidewise, sidewinder, sidereal, sleeping, snaking in
grass in Nike sneakers, a sting, *aswirl* (you might say)
predator advantage, blind prey, can you pre-date your
mate, go past best-before and be safe

Cracks in the chamber, greenhouse fires, airless news-chatter smash and grab acts, all hail to the voluble, bee-essing banker the high-wire walker cabling his wealth offshore—all the torn pages shorn lives, testaments testimonials, the spreadsheets, the lies

Let nature's enjambed database weep, *en plein air*, let the complainants raise funds for lawyers, let lawyers grow rich by compliments on their suits, while bypassing security lineups fidgeting mobiles upgrading their seats before boarding

Tears comb over cheeks, wash off war paint it's retrograde, reverse arrow murmuration, our flocking instinct lost, willingly released and advertised . . . *arrowheads by actual Indians MADE IN INDIA*

Authentic goes spurious, the spear's a fraud while fraudsters grin on nightly news razored payoff shreds liminal attention, libidinal limbs flinch, shudder, teeth mince air, spit quince, unwritten thought, the un-bowed word strums the veritable bovine undercurrent rhizomatic

Uprise versatile verse, all we can say and keep saying to keep sane

PLAITED

Slumbered pair, breathing history
      into strands of each other's hair

Puffed breath-paced ripples
      in plaited, fated sheets

Pulse beats tick-tock-clock
      heart's soft bud-up bud-up bud-up bud-up

Blind hands drift toward the other's warmth
      clock hands circling to appointed

Bed's embrace, tucked edges, limit time's bruise
      blue night skin quivers, alive, touched, untouchable

Night-seam between nothing and will-be
      palm to palm, a leaf turns, anticipating light

An eye opens, as bud to bloom, stirs
      another eye, like a light-year leap

Out of sleep, a kiss, a lick
      faces flush, haloed in pale sheets

Bodies braid, a damp lock
      of skin-held milk-blue veins

In the bunched ruffle, an aftershock breaks
      behind them, cramps them, burns

STAGED

i.

Comes toward you, unexpected
shape unfamiliar, upon you, a limping gait
in staged haste, a grind, a wrestle of
knees, elbows, wrists
a *sh-sh-sh* that trails
behind bony-fingered flails

ii.

The room echoes, a joke unheard
stop or go flashes
solid or pliant, splintered in descent's
flare, reshaped
as mask

iii.

Moth, fated to flare's
smoke-knotted hiss
wind-whisper, ashen, lifts
above blind brightness

Siren, lipsticked, sears
the road's crisis, weaves, whines
braids night's
kisses into distant
echoes

iv.

With light's failure
inhibitions drift to
danger, beckon shadows

A hand snags on fabric
a tug
into fate

v.

Sharp song in memory's throat
forays choral air's notation
a fanfare scheme recalls
a scrawled note
sings
knowing's lamentation

vi.

Sorrow's caked eyes
a tear-salted line
limes a cheek

A probing tongue cannot moisten
cannot soften the inescapable
scab

vii.

A man sits
his last posture
a hand in his throat

Hugged, he heaves, tries to rise
almost laughs at the unheard
punchline

viii.

Sharp barb spikes

Vein-caught clot
pins

ix.

In reversed binocular
the distant story flares
too tiny, too tired
to bear
its dual light

PRISMATIC

i. (the bet)

Word-dazzle, OR word-
                       shade cuddles, cavorts
unwraps a long soft scarf
that snaps
brushes a face in the breeze
it stretches back
far as eye can read
or whips ahead
into unknown
(the oval's overcrowded)

Which way
cast your bet?

Some thoroughbreds you might consider
Single-Tongued Lick-Link
OR *Mouthful of Words*
OR take a flier on the Daily Double
Verses' Voice
and *Trouble Your Mirror*

      Beyond the raked dirt, the white rail
      OR in a cinema's back row a tender whisper *kiss me*
      OR at a fireplace flame, warm
      lips mouth Sarah Vaughan's *September Song*
      its *waiting game*, until . . .
      a throat, at the bell, screams *GO, GO!*

Over pounding hooves
the pen-scribble
the churned up muddy track
(in the stands a quick sup of currency)

It's Seduction
it's Jazz
it's the Speed of things

Sounds like Futurism
looks like Charades

At the finish line in a clutch
a shutter-snap

A word flares
the poem exchanges the win for a vowel, OR
vice versa, OR
not

Hero-poet bathes in wreathed light
OR weathers in his cups

ii. (*evidence*)

Double
OR nothing
OR almost (daily)
hard
      -hearted OR
      -assed
           OR half-

What's the differential (reverential)?

Speed tracked
OR handy-packed

How to see light
that flares?

A cruel death
OR angry scare
      religion not withstanding—or upstanding—yes, unsettling
OR even scarred
      nodding off (for weariness
OR loss of blood)
      blood's reward, a visceral ooze
      a ragged cut that seeps a poem, perhaps

OR a fixated traveller who wanders thought
      dips, winds, listens to
      a whisper, back row, dark cinema
OR in a song   OR to a mirror

Single-tongued link   OR layered
leaping ahead   to ink-scritched views contesting
the inarguable
photo finish evidence (the *I was there*)
freezing the palimpsest

OR as far as the eye can read
against all odds
the hoarse-voiced race to the last word

iii. *(exposure)*

Dazzle   the dazed line starts
whips words
phrases
stretches out
the read
leaps with unexpected pace
syllable-tailed single-tongued bursts
headlong into furlong
wrought song

Iambic triactor
back row, dark cinema, whisper and kiss

Horserace photo finish snap re-
frames the moment's hope, its monumental
inarguable evidence, by a nose
betting-window shout, *fuck! faux-pas!*
          shsh!

                    scritch/script   inkdip
                              wind
     wanders
               curve   of a thought
          knots into poem's complex, selective
          rhymes, its thoroughbred crimes, OR

          Offtrack, meanders in sentences, seeks story's revel
          characters in trouble, wounds that seep
          blood, lost bets, lost haul
          hall of mirrors

(How does a pen, a shutter, do that?)

No nodding off!

> See—the plausible reigns
> probability's odds die
> an angry scowl
> *Aha*!

> See—the caught light
> flares across plight's screen
> doubled   OR   naught

SPLINTER

i.

Rock fulcrum
plank balance
creaks, crumbles, lets
go its authority
hat socked over eyes
you tilt your chin to the flow's
streaming negative refill
the spreadsheet formula knot
a table set

ii.

Paper-white knuckles
at the breakup, knocked on splinters
at the edge of ice's ness where
chill dislodges
any promise of
(say, tilling, leafing out)
the plank, a buckle, the
cautious door

A snapshot kiss on retina's
acetate sheet-shimmer
withholds the undertaking, the image faint
where fear quakes

If you lean, will it
not tear
beneath you

iii.

Scissors situate you between
slice and trim
between one and two
hold and fall
despite your faith, your
hope, your jewelry's
otherly sheen

The formula screen snaps shut
behind, you can't reach back, clutch
the game's hand, the tools
risk's allure has been
dealt, you resist
the fixed portrait that shows
what's back there, that
stutters your hands
clamps to your legs
and the flow
and over you
darkness, over
you, lowering

grasping roots on the slope of the voice

—Michel Deguy

NOTES ON SOURCES

Absence is a door / that all pass through / the I that opens to a you

—Fred Wah

The source poems that seeded this work and then disappeared back into their own lives are listed below. There has been no intention to imitate or trace, but rather to simply leap off an edge that each source provided.

Chirrup
On "Snapshot of a Crease," Oana Avasilichioaei. From *Abandon,* Wolsak and Wynn, Don Mills, ON. 2005. p.40.

Rush
On "The Room's Penumbra," Coral Bracho (trans. Forrest Gander). From *Firefly Under the Tongue: Selected Poems of Coral Bracho*. New Directions, New York. 2008. p.41.

Tailwind
i. On "Nine River Ghazals #2," Di Brandt. From *Walking to Mojácar,* Turnstone Press, Winnipeg. 2010. p.6.

ii. Transcreation:
On *Neuf ghazals pour la rivière* #2, Di Brandt. From *Walking to Mojácar,* Turnstone Press, Winnipeg. 2010. p.7.

Slip
On "YOU FORGET," Paul Celan (trans. Nikolai Popov and Heather McHugh). From *Glottal Stop: 101 Poems,* Wesleyan University Press, Middletown, CT. 2000. p.31.

ZigZag
On "Sonnet: I Am," John Clare. From "I Am": *The Selected Poetry of John Clare*, Farrar Straus and Giroux. New York. 2003. p.283.

Oxygen
On "Breaking the Lines," Hilary Clark. From *The Dwelling of Weather*, Brick Books. London, ON. 2003. p.95.

Slender
On "tidings," Dennis Cooley. From *Sunfall: New and Selected Poems, 1980–1996*, Anansi. Toronto. 1996. p.168.

Laden
i. On "Blow of Silence," Michel Deguy. From *Given Giving*, University of California Press. Berkeley and Los Angeles. 1984. p.151.

ii. On "The Wall," Michel Deguy. From *Given Giving*, University of California Press, Berkeley and Los Angeles, 1984. p.153.

Witness
On "Winter, #100," Paulette Dubé. From *Gaits*, Thistledown Press, Saskatoon, SK. 2010. p.63.

Aslant
On "Nocturne," Sarah Gridley. From *Weather Eye Open*, University of California Press, Berkeley and Los Angeles. 2005. p.31.

Water-Song
On "THE DAY CELAN SAW ANTSCHEL IN THE SEINE," Phil Hall. From *An Oak Hunch*, Brick Books, London, ON. 2005. p.74.

Repertoire
In Memory of Bernard Heidsieck
On "PARTITION V: le quatrième plan," Bernard Heidsieck. From
Partition V: poèmes-partition, Le Soleil Noir. Paris. 1973. pp.58–62

Agora
On "#3," Lyn Hejinian. From *The Guard,* Tuumba Press. Berkeley.
1984. Unpaginated.

Pent
On "#3," Robert Kroetsch. From *The Seed Catalogue* (illustrated ed.),
Red Deer Press. Red Deer, AB. 2004. pp.13–15.

Spiderish
On "Island of Prosections 1," Sylvia Legris. In *The Hideous Hidden.*
(Unpublished, 2012).

Peck
Transcreation:
On "Pequeño poema infinito," Federico García Lorca. From *Selected
Verse,* Farrar, Straus and Giroux, New York. 1994. p.296.

North
On "The Same Language " in *Winter Music: Composing in the North,*
John Luther Adams. Wesleyan University Press, Middletown, CT.
2004. pp. Various.

Offering
On Daphne Marlatt. Source poem reference lost.

Dis(re)covery
For Roy Miki
On "Material Recovery Eleven," Roy Miki. From *Surrender,* The
Mercury Press, Toronto. 2001. pp.118–119.

Allure
On "Relief," Richard Miles. From *Boat of Two Shores,* University of
Maine at Machias Press, Machias, ME. 2007. pp.14–15.

Decoy
On "unfinished song & change (changing)," bpNichol. From *The Other
Side of the Room: Poems, 1966–69,* Weed/Flower Press, Toronto. 1971.
pp.16–17.

Tumble
On "Now that I live in Stockholm," Charles Noble. From *The Kindness
Colder Than the Elements.* Au Press, Edmonton. 2011. p.127.

Lurch
On "Battle Cry," Lisa Robertson. From *Debbie: An Epic.* New Star
Books, Vancouver. 1997. Lines 655–685.

Olives
On *Elucidata*, Mari-Lou Rowley. From *The Fungi Among Us,* in *Viral
Suite.* Anvil Press, Vancouver. 2004. p.58.

Petals
On *Parterres* in *mortar rake glove sausan broom basin sansui,* Gerry
Shikatani. From *First Book, Three Gardens of Andalucía. The Capilano
Review, Series 2, No. 39/40,* Vancouver. 2003. pp.78–80.

Glory

On "Whirlpool," Jennifer Still. From *Girlwood*, Brick Books, London, ON. 2011. p.57.

Arrows

On "Muttersprache 1972/2: Material Resistance," Ulf Stolterfoht (trans. Rosemarie Waldrop). From *Lingos I-IX*, Burning Deck, Providence, RI. 2006. p.77.

Plaited

On "The Mirror," Shu Ting (trans. F. Dai, D. Ding, and E. Morin). From *Poetry for the Millennium, Volume Two* (ed. J. Rothenberg and P. Joris), University of California Press, Berkeley and Los Angeles. 1998. p.762.

Staged
In memory of Richard Truhlar
On "Moon Dice," Richard Truhlar. Underwhich Editions, Toronto. 1982. All poems, Unpaginated.

Prismatic
On "20 (comet)," Fred Wah. From *Articulations,* in *Sentenced to Light.* Talonbooks, Vancouver. 2008. p.122.

Splinter
On "Blasted Hymn," Elizabeth Willis. From *Address.* Wesleyan University Press, Middletown, CT. 2011. p.41.

ADDITIONAL CITATIONS

Inscription 1
Michel Deguy. In *L'effacement*. From *Recumbents*, Wesleyan University Press, Middletown, CT. 2005. p.78.

Postscript 1
Michel Deguy. In *Projet de livre des gisants; Mouvement pertpétuel.* From *Recumbents*, (trans. Wilson Baldridge.) Wesleyan University Press, Middletown, CT. 2005. p.27.

Postscript 2
Fred Wah. In *Medallions of Belief.* BookThug, Toronto. 2012. p.37.

ACKNOWLEDGMENTS

I acknowledge sources, provokers, locations, and modes that have enabled and influenced this work. Each poet writes with and among many. I have attempted to honour this reality.

I am grateful for the studio spaces in the Leighton Colony at The Banff Centre. There I've worked in a fishing boat, a snail shell, and a cathedral, looking into the pines. On Galiano Island, British Columbia, I've worked at a picnic table facing Active Pass and Georgia Strait and in an unserviced cabin looking out at the fall rains and towering fir and cedar trees. At Willowbend, a country home by the Bow River near Carseland, I polished this work into its final form. These settings, among others, account for the openings and closings and formations, turbulent or calm, found herein.

Thank you to publishers of print, digital, audio, and video formats, who have given space to earlier versions of the *Emanations* poems: *Contemporary Verse 2*; *FreeFall*; *Rampike*; *Vallum*; *West Coast Line*; *Where Nights Are Twice As Long* (anthology); *Forget* (online); "The Road Home" (CKUA-Radio); and *Link Up With Canadian Poetry* (Parliamentary Poet Laureate video project).

I deeply appreciate the fluttering emanations that all these relationships provide.

ABOUT THE AUTHOR

Steven Ross Smith is a sound and performance poet who also works in fiction and non-fiction. He has served as publisher/editor at Underwhich Editions, business manager of *Grain* magazine, managing editor for Banff Centre Press, and as editor of the online magazine *Boulderpavement*. He has been publishing books since the 1970s, and was a member of the legendary sound poetry group, Owen Sound. He has also written two librettos. Smith's book *fluttertongue 3: disarray* won the 2005 Saskatchewan Book of the Year Award. The chapbook *Pliny's Knickers*, a collaboration between Smith, poet Hilary Clark, and artist Betsy Rosenwald, won the 2006 bpNichol Chapbook Award. He was the founding Director of Sage Hill Writing Experience and ran the program from 1990 to 2007. In 2008, he became Director of Literary Arts at The Banff Centre, where he served until March 2014. Smith currently lives and writes in Banff, Alberta and on Galiano Island, British Columbia.

COLOPHON

Manufactured as the first edition of *Emanations* by
BookThug in the fall of 2015. Distributed in Canada by
the Literary Press Group: www.lpg.ca. Distribibuted in
the US by Small Press Distribution: www.spdbooks.org.

Shop online at www.bookthug.ca

BOOK
PRODUCTION
WAR ECONOMY
STANDARD

Type + design by Jay MillAr
Edited for the press by Phil Hall
Copy edited by Ruth Zuchter

-like

sideways
side-

is   a-swirl/

sses.

yalty   combine

le grace

en phar

splade 1972/2:
il Resistance"
of
. 2006

the Cam

No promise is
adequate, though
there's

it's folly

tly adult-like

sideways, sidewise,
side-winder

meadow's
chid grasses.

a-swirl (you might say

nee to royalty

coupling, de grace

combined with spo

, the chamber
of indifference

en plein air

hyming thought
nnot be stopped;
blime

a workshop, all the
pages, the green
fires,
let not